THE POWER
OF YOUR

THOUGHTS

THIS JOURNAL BELONGS TO

_____

Published in the United States by:
Hay House, Inc.: www.hayhouse.com®
Published in Australia by:
Hay House Australia Pty. Ltd.: www.hayhouse.com.au
Published in the United Kingdom by:
Hay House UK, Ltd.: www.hayhouse.co.uk
Published in India by:
Hay House Publishers India: www.hayhouse.co.in

Cover and interior design: Julie Davison

Tradepaper ISBN: 978-1-4019-7252-3

10 9 8 7 6 5 4 3 2 1
1st edition, May 2024

Printed in China

LOUISE HAY

THE POWER OF YOUR

THOUGHTS

A GUIDED JOURNAL
for Self-Empowerment

HAY HOUSE, INC.
Carlsbad, California • New York City
London • Sydney • New Delhi

INTRODUCTION

LOUISE HAY was certainly one of the most empowered people we knew, and she embodied everything we try to do here at Hay House. She wasn't always like this, though: Her early life was filled with poverty and abuse, and it took her many years to feel anything close to self-esteem. Ultimately, she did learn to love herself, and it was important to her that others could benefit from her experiences. She did not think she was special and was fond of saying, "If *I* can do it, anyone can."

We believe this is true. Her words of wisdom helped countless people while she was with us, and we are grateful to still be able to share them now that she's gone. This journal contains her timeless teachings on every page, presented in a new way. As you actively participate in the exercises, you will learn to take the reins of your life in a positive, loving way. We hope you will then share that love and sense of empowerment with those around you and beyond. In this way, Louise's vision of a world in which we are safe to love one another will continue to be realized.

May this journal help you use the power of your thoughts to manifest the life of your dreams!

— THE HAY HOUSE EDITORS

Life loves me and wants me to be happy.

YOU ARE MEANT TO BE a wonderful, loving expression of Life, which is waiting for you to open up to it—to feel worthy of the good it holds for you. Life wants you to have the very best. Life wants you to have peace of mind, inner joy, confidence, and an abundance of self-worth and self-love. You deserve to feel at ease at all times with all people. The wisdom and intelligence of the Universe is yours to use, and you are always loved and supported.

Trust the power within you to be there for you.

We are in the midst of enormous individual and global change. I believe that all of us who are living at this time chose to be here to be a part of these changes, to bring about change, and to transform the world from the old way of life to a more loving and peaceful existence. Once upon a time, we looked "out there" for our savior, but now we are learning to go within to find it. We are the power we have been seeking. We are in charge of our lives.

We are powerful, creative beings who determine our future with every thought we think and every word we speak. When we have illumination, when we become conscious of what we are doing, we can begin to change our lives.

We are all responsible for every experience in our lives, the best and the worst. We create these experiences by the thoughts we think and the words we speak. It is very important to understand this point:

We have the power of our thoughts and words. As we change our thinking and our words, our experiences also change.

No matter where we came from, no matter how difficult our childhood was, we can make positive changes today.

When we begin to take conscious charge of our thoughts and words, then we have tools we can use to create the life of our dreams. That's what this journal is about. You will discover many exercises throughout, and it is important that you take your time with each one. There is no time limit here, nor is there any need to rush the process, and you'll want to make sure you get as much out of this journal as you can. (There are extra pages in the back if you need more room to write for any of the entries.) A few meditations are also included, and you may want to record them first so that you can close your eyes and have the full experience. Finally, I'd like to encourage you to flex your creative muscles throughout the process, so that your mind, heart, and soul are all engaged and working together for the most authentic result for you.

Life is really here for you.
You need only ask.

Tell Life what you want, and then allow the good to happen. By the time you have finished with the book, it is my hope that you will have felt the truth of the quote above and know how truly empowered you are.

Empowerment is
teaching myself to fly . . .
and I know my
wings are strong!

AS WE BEGIN, I'd like you to write down how you feel about your life right now. What areas do you feel are going well, and what could use some improvement? What do you really want?

_____

_____

_____

_____

_____

_____

_____

Next, think about the concept of power: Do you feel you have it in your life? Who or what do you feel has power in the world? Have there been times you have felt especially empowered? Was that comfortable for you or not? Did you grow up in a home or culture that emphasized personal power? Record your answers below.

_____

_____

_____

_____

_____

_____

_____

Many of us were not raised feeling empowered; in fact, lots of us were encouraged to be as small and meek as possible. In many cultures, for example, women are expected to give their power to men.

I remember a woman once telling me that she was not assertive because that was the way she was brought up. It took years for her to realize that her conditioning kept her locked in a corner. She particularly blamed her husband and her in-laws for her problems. Eventually, she divorced her husband, yet she still blamed him for so many things that were not right in her life. It took her 10 years to relearn her patterns and take her power back. In hindsight, she realized that *she* was responsible for not speaking up and for not standing up for herself, not her husband or her in-laws. They were there to reflect back to her what she felt inside—a sense of powerlessness.

If this resonates with you, understand that the time has come to make a change.

You no longer need to give your power over to anyone else's pictures of right and wrong.

Remember, they only have power over you when you give your power to them.

No person, place,
or thing has any
power over me.
I am free.

This is the
moment I take
my power back!

IF OUR LIVES ARE UNHAPPY, or if we are feeling unfulfilled, it's easy to blame someone else and say it's all *their* fault. Is there someone you blame for the circumstances of your life? Write about this below.

_____

_____

_____

_____

_____

_____

_____

_____

_____

_____

_____

_____

_____

_____

_____

_____

_____

_____

Understand that words of blame will not bring us freedom. Rather, they keep us stuck in our conditions, our problems, and our frustrations.

Our power comes from taking responsibility for our lives.

I know it sounds scary to be responsible for our lives, but we absolutely are, whether we accept it or not. Blame is about giving away our power. Responsibility gives us the power to make changes in our lives. If we play the victim role, then we are using our personal power to be helpless. If we decide to accept responsibility, then we don't waste time blaming someone or something *out there*. Some people choose to interpret responsibility as guilt. They feel guilty because they believe that they have failed in some way, and it serves to make themselves "wrong." That is not what I'm talking about.

If we can use our challenges as opportunities to think about how we can change our lives, we have power. Some people who face significant health issues, for instance, are able to find things to appreciate in the situation, saying it gave them a chance to go about their lives differently. Other people go around saying, "I'm a victim, woe is me." Those people are going to have a difficult time handling their problems at all, let alone seeing them as opportunities for empowerment.

Responsibility is our ability to respond to a situation.

We always have a choice. It does not mean that we deny whatever is happening in our lives. It merely means that we can acknowledge that we have contributed to where we are. By taking responsibility, we have the power to change. We can say, "What can *I* do here?" We need to understand that we all have personal power *all the time*. We can always decide to react differently than we have so far.

Our circumstances may not change, but we have the power to change, forever.

So, returning to the earlier exercise, how can you shift your feelings of blame to those of responsibility? How can you take your power back here?

_____

_____

_____

_____

_____

_____

_____

_____

_____

_____

_____

_____

_____

_____

_____

_____

_____

_____

_____

_____

_____

The point of power is in the present moment.

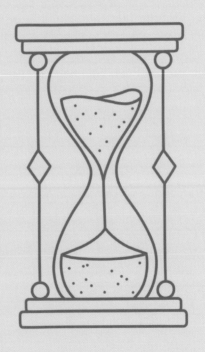

THE PAST ONLY EXISTS IN OUR MINDS and in the way we choose to look at it in our minds. *This* is the moment we are living. *This* is the moment we are feeling. *This* is the moment we are experiencing. What we are doing right now is laying the groundwork for tomorrow. So *this* is the moment to make the decision. We can't do anything tomorrow, and we can't do anything yesterday. We can only do it today.

> What is important is what we are choosing to think, believe, and say *right now.*

It doesn't matter how long we've had a negative pattern or an illness or a poor relationship or lack of abundance or no sense of purpose. We can start to make a shift today. The thoughts we've held and the words we've repeatedly used have created our life and experiences up to this point.

Yet that is past thinking; we've already done that. What we're choosing to think and say today, at this moment, will create tomorrow and the next day and the next week and the next month and the next year, and so on. The point of power is always in the present moment. This is where we begin to make changes. What a liberating idea! We can begin to let the old nonsense go. Right now. The smallest beginning will make a difference.

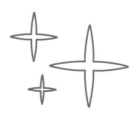

Although all the events we have experienced up to this moment have been created by our thoughts and beliefs from the past, let's not look back on our lives with shame. Instead, let's see the past as part of the richness and fullness of our life. Without this richness and fullness, we would not be here today. There is no reason to beat ourselves up because we didn't do better. We did the best we knew how.

How do you feel about this? Explore your reaction below.

_____

_____

_____

_____

_____

_____

_____

_____

_____

_____

_____

_____

_____

No matter where you are in life, no matter what you've contributed to creating, no matter what's happening, you are always doing the best you can with the understanding and awareness and knowledge that you have. And when you know more, you will do it differently. Don't berate yourself for where you are. Don't blame yourself for not doing it faster or better.

Be patient with yourself. From the moment you decide to make a change, until you see the results of your efforts, you may vacillate from the old to the new. Don't get angry with yourself. You want to build yourself up, not beat yourself up.

You need your own loving support if you want to make changes.

Understand that you're not a bad person for thinking the way you have so far. You just never learned *how* to think and talk. Your parents probably didn't know this, so they couldn't possibly teach it to you. They taught you how to look at life in the way that *their* parents taught them. So nobody is *wrong*.

Just because we've believed something negative about ourselves or about our lives does not mean that there is any truth to it. As children, we heard negative things about ourselves and life, and we accepted these ideas as if they were true. We are now going to examine the things we've believed and make a decision to either continue to believe them, because they support us and make our life joyful and fulfilled, or release them.

This is a time of awakening.

It is time for you to consciously create your life in a way that pleases and supports you. Know that you are always safe. It may not seem so at first, but you will learn that Life is always there for you. You are about to reach for new habits that use your thoughts and energy in a more productive way.

You can do it!

I know that I can create
miracles in my life.
I accept my power.

WHAT KIND OF THOUGHTS make you feel good? Thoughts of love, appreciation, gratitude, joyful childhood experiences? Thoughts in which you rejoice that you're alive and bless your body with love? Do you truly enjoy this present moment and get excited about tomorrow? Thinking these kinds of thoughts is an act of loving yourself, and loving yourself creates miracles in your life.

Life is very simple:
Whatever we give out, we get back.

In other words, if we want a joyous life, we must think joyous thoughts. If we want a prosperous life, we must think prosperous thoughts. If we want a loving life, we must think loving thoughts.

Whatever we send out mentally or
verbally will come back to us in like form.

Yet so many of us move through life on autopilot, not consciously aware of the thousands of thoughts that go through our heads every day.

Let's take a close look now at the power of your thoughts. Imagine yourself in line at a cafeteria, or perhaps at a buffet in a luxurious hotel, where instead of dishes of food, there are dishes of thoughts. You get to choose any and all that you wish, and these thoughts will create your future experiences.

Now, if you choose thoughts that will create problems and pain, that's rather foolish. It's like choosing food that always makes you ill. You may do this once or twice, but as soon as you learn which foods upset your body, you'll stay away from them. It's the same with thoughts—stay away from the ones that create problems and pain, and choose the ones that make you feel good.

In order to do this, however, you need to become aware of what is currently taking up space in your head. It can be challenging to pay attention to every single thought, so try this exercise: For the next week, take 10 minutes at the same time every day to do some automatic writing. Simply put pen to paper and record whatever is coming up, without editing or criticism. (Use separate paper or the pages in the back of this journal, if needed.) Think of yourself like a reporter, noting what's happening without judgment.

_____

_____

_____

_____

_____

_____

_____

_____

_____

_____

_____

_____

_____

_____

_____

_____

When the week is done, review what you've written and note any similar thoughts or themes. For example, if you notice that you jotted down being tired or busy several times, write that down. Describe what you observed here.

_____

_____

_____

_____

_____

_____

_____

_____

_____

_____

_____

_____

_____

_____

_____

_____

_____

_____

_____

_____

OUR THOUGHTS SPEED THROUGH our minds very quickly, so it is difficult to shape them at first. Our mouths, on the other hand, are slower. We can begin right now to watch and listen to what we say.

There is tremendous power in our spoken words, and many of us are not aware of just how important they are. Let us consider words as the foundation of what we continually create in our lives. We use words all the time, yet we babble away, seldom paying attention to the ones we use.

Much like recording our thoughts, recording what we say is a helpful exercise. You can get started by using a voice recorder or your phone. For the next week, push the record button every time you make or receive a call, or have a conversation (with the other person's permission, of course). When the week is over, listen to what you said and how you said it. You will probably be amazed as you hear the words you use and the inflection of your voice. If you find that you said something three times or more, note that this is a pattern. Some of the patterns may be positive and supportive, but you may have some negative patterns that you repeat over and over again as well.

What did you discover about the words you often use? What were your positive patterns? And what were your negative ones?

_____

_____

_____

_____

_____

_____

_____

_____

_____

_____

_____

_____

_____

_____

_____

_____

_____

_____

_____

_____

I only speak words
that are loving,
positive, and
constructive.

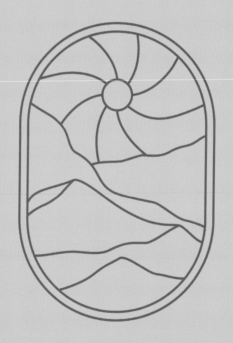

SHOULD IS A WORD that my ear is particularly attuned to. It is as if a bell goes off every time I hear it. Often, I will hear people use a dozen *should*s in a paragraph. These same people wonder why their lives are so rigid or why they can't move out of a situation. They want control over things that they cannot control. They are either making themselves wrong or making someone else wrong. And then they question why they aren't living lives of freedom and empowerment.

I believe that *should* is one of the most damaging words in our language. Every time we use it, we are, in effect, saying "wrong." Either we are wrong, or we were wrong, or we are going to be wrong. I would like to take the word *should* out of our vocabulary forever, and replace it with the word *could*. *Could* empowers us because it gives us choice, and we are never wrong.

Think of five things that you "should" do.

I should:

_____

_____

_____

_____

_____

_____

_____

_____

_____

_____

Now replace *should* with *could*.

I could:

_____

_____

_____

_____

_____

_____

_____

_____

Finally, ask yourself, "Why haven't I?" You may find that you have been berating yourself for years for something that you never wanted to do in the first place or for something that was never your idea. How many *should*s can you drop from your list?

_____

_____

_____

_____

_____

_____

_____

We can remove the expression *have to* from our vocabulary and our thinking as well. When we do, we will release a lot of self-imposed pressure on ourselves. We create tremendous stress by saying, "I have to go to work. I have to do this. I have to . . . I have to . . ." Instead, let's begin to say, *choose to*: "I choose to go to work because it pays the rent right now." *Choose to* offers a whole different perspective on our lives and brings the power back to us.

How can you replace *have to* with *choose to* in your own life?

_____

_____

_____

_____

_____

_____

_____

_____

_____

_____

_____

_____

_____

_____

_____

The beauty of awareness is that it interrupts a pattern. Bringing attention to our conversations—the things we say either out loud or to ourselves every single day—is a way of becoming present to the truth. The messages we give ourselves day in and day out deepen a groove in the mind, giving them more power. And they also transmit energy out into the world, drawing back to us the very thing we focus on.

Keep in mind that feelings of inadequacy start with negative thoughts that we have about ourselves. However, these thoughts have no power over us unless we act upon them. Thoughts are only words strung together. They have no meaning whatsoever, unless we give them meaning. We tend to believe the worst about ourselves, focusing on the negative messages over and over again in our minds.

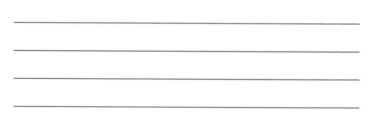

The truth is, we're always perfect, always beautiful, and ever-changing.

We're doing the best we can with the understanding, knowledge, and awareness we have. As we grow and change more and more, our "best" will only get better and better.

What can you do to bring more awareness into your life? What reminders can you set for yourself to check in with your thoughts and emotions?

_____

_____

_____

_____

_____

_____

_____

I recognize that awareness is the first step in healing or changing. I become more aware with each passing day.

I now choose to
look for the good
wherever I am.
I do this with people,
with places, and
with situations.

HUMANS HAVE A "NEGATIVITY BIAS," which means that we are more apt to be drawn to bad news. Too many of us keep recycling negative stories until we believe that there is only bad in the world. I have found it to be the case that so many people don't want to hear good news because they prefer to have something to complain about.

When you are around other people, begin to listen to what they say and how they say it. See if you can connect what they say with what they are experiencing in life. What else do you notice? Does the way they talk make you feel good, for instance, or do you find yourself wanting to pull away from the negativity? Does it seem empowering? Explore your findings here.

_____

_____

_____

_____

_____

_____

_____

_____

_____

_____

_____

_____

_____

_____

NEGATIVITY GREATLY IMPACTS social media too. It is well known that the negativity bias results in more clicks and shares; it is equally well known that this activity contributes to poor mental health and self-esteem. It also serves to keep us distracted from the voice of our true self, which contributes to our feelings of powerlessness.

Write about your experiences with social media below. In what ways has it had a negative impact on your self-worth?

_____

_____

_____

_____

_____

_____

Does it seem like it might be time to make a change here? If so, what is your more empowering plan?

_____

_____

_____

_____

_____

_____

_____

I now arise from
the negativity
of the past.
I am free to
live a new life.

I look within
to find my
treasures.

MANY YEARS AGO, I learned to pay attention to what I call my *inner ding*, that place of intuition that is often referred to as *the voice within*. I trust the voice of my true self implicitly because when that ding goes *Yes!*—even if it seems like a crazy choice—I know that it's right for me. My inner ding has never let me down. Whenever I've gone against it, I've regretted it.

Most of us have a gut feeling about something from time to time, and sadly end up ignoring it or having others talk us out of it. We really need to stop doing that.

You must learn to trust yourself.

It doesn't matter what you do in this world. It doesn't matter if you are a CEO or a retiree, a homemaker or a dealmaker. You have wisdom inside of you that is connected to Universal Truth. When you look within and ask a simple question such as, "What is this experience trying to teach me?" and are willing to listen, then you will have the answer.

Most of us are so busy running around creating the soap opera and drama we call our lives, or distracting ourselves with negative pursuits, that we don't hear anything. Yet the inner ding is the honest, authentic voice of our soul, and listening to it is the key to empowerment.

Now is the time to go within and learn about your own power and what you are capable of doing. Listen to your own voice—it will always steer you through life in the best possible way for you.

We all have a treasure trove of wisdom,
peace, love, and joy inside of us—
and they are only a breath away.

All we have to do to connect with these gifts is to close our eyes, take a deep breath, and tune in to ourselves.

Our breath is the most precious substance in our lives, and yet we totally take it for granted that when we exhale, our next breath will be there. If we didn't take another breath, we wouldn't last three minutes. Now, if the power that created us has given us enough breath to last as long as we shall live, can't we have faith that everything else we need will also be supplied?

It is helpful to become aware of your breath as it flows in and out of your body. We often hold our breath when we are frightened, for example, so be sure to focus on breathing evenly. When you become physically frightened, your adrenaline pumps through your body to protect you from danger. It's the same with the fear you manufacture in your mind.

Breathing helps you tap into your power.

It straightens your spine. It opens your chest and gives your heart room to expand. By breathing, you begin to drop the barriers and open up. You expand rather than contract. Your love flows. It is all there within you, and no one can ever take it from you. No matter what is going on in your life, you can always take a moment to focus on your breath and reconnect with yourself.

Take a few minutes now to just sit and breathe. Imagine that as you inhale, you are drawing in the power of the Universe, filling you with love, protection, and security. As you exhale, imagine you are expelling all of your worries, insecurities, and negativity.

When you're ready, journal about how this exercise made you feel.

_____

_____

_____

_____

_____

_____

_____

_____

_____

_____

_____

_____

_____

_____

_____

_____

_____

_____

_____

All that I seek is
already within me.

ALL THE ANSWERS TO all the questions we will ever ask are already within us. We just need to take the time to connect to them. That's why meditation is so vital—it quiets us down so that we can hear our own inner wisdom. No one can be completely in touch with the abundance of knowledge within without taking time each day to meditate.

Sitting in silence is one of the most valuable things we can do. No one out there knows more about our life, or what is best for us, than we do, right here inside.

> Our inner wisdom is the best direct connection we have with all of life.

We are always connected to this guidance and do not need to chase after it. We just need to create the opportunity for it to come to us.

To me, meditation is when we sit down and turn off our self-talk long enough to hear that guidance. Meditation can come in many ways, so like all things in your life, doing what works best for you will be most beneficial. If you do just a bit of research, you'll find many great options to try.

When I meditate, I usually close my eyes, take a deep breath, and ask: "What is it I need to know?" Then I sit and listen. I might also ask, "What is it I need to learn?" or "What is the lesson in this?" Sometimes, we think we're supposed to fix everything in our lives, and maybe we're really only supposed to learn something from the situation.

Try this now. Take five minutes to close your eyes, sit in silence, and ask yourself, "What is it I need to know?" Write down the message you receive.

_____

_____

_____

_____

_____

_____

_____

_____

_____

_____

_____

_____

_____

_____

_____

When I first began to meditate, it was so unfamiliar and against all my usual inner programming that I had violent headaches the first three weeks. Nevertheless, I hung in there, and the headaches eventually disappeared. Similarly, if you are constantly coming up with a tremendous amount of negativity when you meditate, it may mean that it *needs* to come up, and when you quiet yourself, it starts to flow to the surface. Simply see the negativity being released. Try not to fight it. Allow it to continue as long as it needs to.

If you fall asleep when you meditate, that's all right. Let the body do what it needs to do; it will balance out in time. The important thing is that you remember to listen to yourself—be sure you consistently give yourself the time and space to hear your inner wisdom.

Over the next few days, write down any messages and feelings that come up for you in meditation. Do you notice any patterns?

_____

_____

_____

_____

_____

_____

_____

_____

_____

_____

_____

WHAT ARE YOUR LAST THOUGHTS before going to bed? Are they powerful healing thoughts or worried, "poverty" thoughts? Note that when I speak of poverty thoughts, I don't mean it in the sense of lack of money. It can be a negative way of thinking about anything—any part of your life that is not flowing freely. In other words, do you worry about tomorrow, keeping yourself up at night?

Understand that consuming any type of news just before you go to sleep takes all that negativity into your dream world. I am so against people doing this!

You need to be mindful of what you're putting into your consciousness before you go to sleep.

I am aware that when I sleep, I am doing a lot of clearing that will prepare me for the next day. I usually read something positive when I go to bed, and I recommend you do the same.

I also find it very helpful to turn over to my dreams any problems or questions I may have. I know my dreams will help me take care of whatever is going on in my life.

For the next few days, try this: Before you go to sleep, write down whatever is troubling you below. Then, when you wake up, jot down anything that came to you in the night.

_____

_____

_____

_____

_____

_____

_____

_____

_____

_____

_____

_____

_____

_____

_____

_____

_____

_____

_____

_____

I release any
limitations based on
old, negative thoughts.
I joyfully look forward
to the future.

REFER BACK TO THE THEMES you noticed when you wrote down your thoughts on page 21. Would you say that these are more on the negative or positive side? Does it seem as if these are themes that have run through your whole life, or did they appear recently? What might be behind your thought patterns? Explore this here.

_____

_____

_____

_____

_____

_____

_____

_____

_____

_____

_____

_____

_____

_____

_____

_____

_____

_____

If you're like most people, you probably wrote down things such as *I'm so tired, I'm too busy, I'm afraid of being broke, I don't want to be sick,* or *I'm scared of winding up alone.* These are all affirmations. Yes, you're using them every moment, whether you know it or not. Every complaint is an affirmation of something you say you don't want in your life. Every time you get angry, you're affirming that you want more anger in your life. Every time you feel like a victim, you're affirming that you want to continue to feel like a victim. If you feel that Life isn't giving you what you want, then it's certain that you will never have the goodies that Life gives to others—that is, until you change the way you think and talk.

> As you've learned, you must retrain your thinking and speaking into positive patterns if you want to feel empowered.

Creating new affirmations opens the door. It's a beginning point on the path to change. In essence, you're saying to your subconscious mind, "I am taking responsibility. I am aware that there is something I can do to change."

When I talk about creating new affirmations, I mean consciously choosing words that will either help eliminate something from your life or help create something new. It is not hard work. It can be a joyous experience as you lift the burden of old negative beliefs and release them back to the nothingness from whence they came.

Affirmations create a focal point that will allow you to begin changing your thinking.

Affirmative statements *go beyond the reality of the present into the creation of the future through the words you use in the now.* When you choose to affirm *I am very prosperous,* you may actually have very little money in the bank at the moment, but what you're doing is planting seeds for future prosperity.

The secret to having your affirmations work quickly and consistently is to prepare an atmosphere in which they can grow.

Each time you repeat them, you're reaffirming the seeds you've planted in the atmosphere of your mind. Things grow much quicker in fertile, rich soil—that's why you want it to be a *happy* atmosphere. It's easier to think in positive affirmations when you feel good, and the more you choose thoughts that make you feel good, the quicker the affirmations work.

IT'S IMPORTANT FOR YOU to always say your affirmations in the *present* tense and without contractions. For example, typical affirmations would start: *"I have . . ."* or *"I am . . ."* If you say, "I am going to . . ." or "I will have . . . ," then your thought stays out there in the future. The Universe takes your thoughts and words very literally and gives you what you say you want. *Always.*

The subconscious mind is straightforward. It has no strategy or designs. What it hears is what it does. If you say, "I don't want to be sick anymore," the subconscious mind hears *sick more.* You have to tell it clearly what you do want. That is: *I am feeling wonderfully well. I radiate good health.*

How often have you lamented what you didn't want? Did it ever bring you what you truly wanted? Fighting the negative is a total waste of time if you honestly want to make changes in your life. The more you dwell on what you don't want, the more of it you create.

> What you put your attention on grows
> and becomes permanent in your life.

Move away from the negative, and focus your attention on what it is that you really do want to be or have.

Saying affirmations is also only part of the process. What you do the rest of the day and night is even more important. Sometimes people will say their affirmations once a day and complain the rest of the time. It will take a long time for affirmations to work if they're done that way. The complaining affirmations will always win, because there are more of them, and they're usually said with great feeling.

So now that you understand a bit more about how powerful your thoughts and words are, are you willing to change your self-talk into positive affirmations?

Let's look again at the negative thoughts *I'm so tired, I'm too busy, I'm afraid of being broke, I don't want to be sick,* and *I'm scared of winding up alone and unhappy.* We can turn each of these into positive affirmations:

I am filled with energy
and enthusiasm.

I have all the time in the world.
Time expands for me.

I am prosperous.

I am totally healthy.

I am filled with love
and affection. I am joyous
and happy and free.

Try it yourself with the statements you wrote on page 45. Remember to write in a way that makes you feel good!

_____

_____

_____

_____

_____

_____

_____

_____

_____

_____

_____

_____

_____

_____

_____

_____

_____

_____

_____

I have the power
to create all that
I wish with my mind
and my thoughts.
I am truly
someone special.

I OFTEN ASK PEOPLE TO LOOK INTO THEIR EYES and say something positive about themselves every time they pass a mirror. These positive statements become even more powerful affirmations through the addition of this "mirror work." The more we use mirrors for complimenting ourselves, approving of ourselves, or supporting ourselves during difficult times, the more we develop a deeper and more enjoyable relationship with ourselves.

The mirror needs to become a companion, a friend instead of an enemy.

Right now I want you to get up. Take this book with you, and find a mirror. Look into your eyes, and say to yourself out loud: "I love you, and I am beginning to make positive changes in my life right now. Day by day I will improve the quality of my life. It is safe for me to be happy and fulfilled." Say this three or four times. Breathe deeply in between.

Notice what thoughts are running through your mind as you make this positive affirmation. Remember that the criticism and negative self-talk is just old chatter. Say to them, "Thank you for sharing." Remember, you can acknowledge your thoughts without giving them power. And don't add to your discomfort by judging yourself for making judgments!

Every time you see a mirror from now on, I want you to look in your eyes and say something positive to yourself. If you are in a hurry, just say "I love you." This simple exercise will produce great results in your life. Write about what's happened after you've done this for a few days.

I give myself
permission to be
all that I can be.
I deserve the
very best in life.

RETURN TO THE LIST YOU MADE ON PAGE 7.

Think about how you answered this question: "What do you really want?" Now say, "I accept for myself _____ [whatever it is you want]." What comes up for you when you do this?

_____

_____

_____

_____

_____

_____

_____

_____

_____

_____

_____

_____

_____

_____

_____

_____

_____

_____

I find that most of us struggle with this exercise. Our personal power stems from the way we perceive our deservability, and we don't believe that we deserve what we really want. Our not deserving comes from childhood messages, but we don't have to feel that we cannot change because of them. Again, we do not want to give our power to other people!

When we don't believe that we deserve good, we will knock the pinnings out from under ourselves, which we can do in a variety of ways: We can create chaos; we can lose things; we can hurt ourselves, have physical problems like falling, or have accidents. We have to start believing that we deserve all the good that Life has to offer.

In order to reprogram the false or negative belief, what would be the first thought that you would need to begin to create this new "whatever" in your life? What would be the building block or the foundation that you would need to stand on? What would be the sort of thing that you would need to know for yourself? To believe? To accept?

Here are some good thoughts to start with:

I am worthwhile.

I am deserving.

I love myself.

I allow myself to be fulfilled.

Can you think of some of your own? Write them here.

_____

_____

_____

_____

_____

_____

_____

_____

_____

_____

_____

_____

_____

_____

_____

_____

_____

_____

_____

_____

_____

These concepts form the very basis of beliefs on which you can build. Repeat your affirmations in addition to these building blocks to create what you want.

I am in awe of
the power of my own
thoughts to heal my
body and my life.

LET'S EXPLORE A FEW SPECIFIC AREAS OF
your life to see how much of a difference empowerment can make. I repeat, *The point of power is always in the present moment.* No matter what you may be dealing with, this is where the changes take place, right here and right now!

First, let's bring our attention to health. Our bodies are amazing. They keep us nurtured and functioning properly, but we must also nurture them back. Remember that our bodies, like everything else in life, mirror our inner thoughts and beliefs. They are always talking to us; we just need to take the time to listen. Every cell within our bodies responds to every single thought we think and every word we speak.

Our emotions travel everywhere in our bodies and affect our organs according to what is going on in our lives. Oftentimes, we are so busy we don't even realize the stress we are putting on ourselves, so getting sick serves as a message to slow down and take a break. Our bodies can tell when something is out of balance, even if it isn't clear in our conscious minds. We must bring our attention to the messages our bodies are giving us!

Take a few minutes to tune in to your body now. What is it telling you?

_____

_____

_____

_____

_____

_____

_____

_____

IF YOU WANT TO CREATE BETTER HEALTH

in your body, you must not get angry at it for any reason. Anger is another affirmation, and it's telling your body that you hate it, or parts of it. Healing means accepting all parts of yourself—not just the parts you like, but *all* of them.

Your body knows how to heal itself. If you nourish it, give it exercise and sufficient sleep, and think positive thoughts, then its work is made easier. The cells are working in a happy atmosphere that's supportive of good health.

Put as much love into your body as you possibly can. Talk to it and stroke it in loving ways. If there's a part of your body that's ailing, then you want to treat it as you would a sick little child. Tell it how much you love it, and that you're doing everything you can to help it get well quickly.

Try these suggestions when you have a chance, and write down how they made you feel.

_____

_____

_____

_____

_____

_____

_____

_____

_____

_____

_____

_____

The more you learn about your health, the easier it is to take care of your body. You don't want to choose to feel like a victim. If you do, you'll just be giving your power away. You don't need to pursue a formal education, but I suggest picking up some books, taking online classes, or talking to supportive health-care workers. Whatever you do, remember to create a healthy, happy mental atmosphere. Also, when exploring healing options, keep in mind that all bodies are different and respond to things differently.

Be a willing participant in your own health plan—after all, true healing involves body, mind, and spirit. So what sounds like an empowering choice for you? When will you take this step?

_____

_____

_____

_____

_____

_____

_____

_____

_____

_____

_____

_____

_____

_____

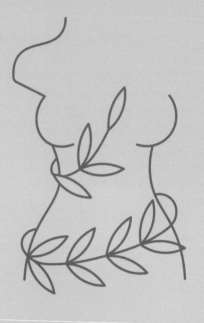

I lovingly do
everything I can
to assist my body
in maintaining
perfect health.

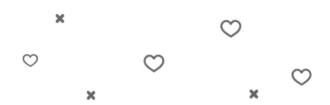

THIS IS A TIME FOR COMPASSION and healing. Go within and connect with that part of yourself that knows how to heal.

You are incredibly
capable and powerful.

Be willing to rise to new levels to find capabilities of which you were not aware, not to just cure dis-ease (my preferred spelling), but to truly heal yourself on all possible levels. To make yourself *whole* in the deepest sense of the word. To accept every part of yourself and every experience you have ever had, and to know that it is all part of the tapestry of your life.

If only we could understand that all of our so-called problems are actually opportunities for us to grow and to change, and that most of them come from the vibrations that we have been giving off! All we really need to do is change the way we think, be willing to dissolve the resentment, and be willing to forgive.

The following meditation can be very helpful for this.

MEDITATION: A RIVER OF FORGIVENESS

Close your eyes and imagine that you have come to a clearing in a lovely meadow, surrounded by majestic mountains. You are inspired by the glorious scenery, and take a deep breath of the clean air.

You notice a rushing stream nearby and head toward it. You have been carrying a lot of baggage, and you set it down once you reach the riverbank.

Some of this baggage contains your old beliefs, which have been holding you back. One by one, let go of them by dropping them into the river. Watch as they gently drift downstream and then totally dissipate and disappear.

Empty the rest of your baggage. Take all the old painful experiences, the hurt, the resentment, and the unforgiveness, and place them in the river. See them begin to dissolve and drift downstream, never to return again.

Take another deep breath of the clean mountain air and relax by the river, no longer surrounded by your baggage.

Reflect on what came up for you when you did this meditation.

_____

_____

_____

_____

_____

_____

_____

_____

I love myself enough to take
excellent care of my body,
and it responds by giving
me vibrant good health.

Here are some additional affirmations I like for health, which you might find helpful:

My healing is already in process.

I listen with love to my body's messages.

I go within and connect with that part of myself that knows how to heal.

I deserve good health.

Try writing down some of your own affirmations here.

_____

_____

_____

_____

_____

_____

_____

_____

_____

_____

_____

_____

_____

_____

_____

_____

_____

_____

_____

_____

_____

_____

_____

_____

_____

_____

Is there anything else you can think of to help you feel empowered about your body? Feel free to write, draw, make a collage, or use any creative tool you like.

_____

_____

_____

_____

_____

_____

_____

_____

_____

_____

_____

_____

_____

_____

_____

_____

_____

_____

_____

_____

I remember that in any relationship I can choose the path that makes me happy, whole, and complete.

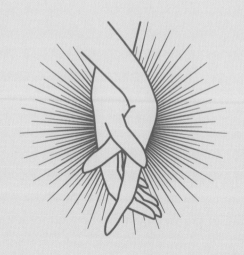

PERSONAL RELATIONSHIPS seem to be the first priority for so many of us. Whether we're looking for romantic or friendly companionship, we don't always attract the right people because our motivations may be unclear. We think, *Oh, if I only had someone who loved me, my life would be so much better.* That's not the way it works. There's a big difference between the need for love and being needy for love.

When you're needy, it means that you're missing love and approval from the most important person you know: yourself. You may become involved in relationships that are co-dependent and ineffectual for both partners.

Particularly when you're first getting to know someone, it can seem natural to almost try to meld with the other person. Yet you must not give your power away, especially at the beginning of a relationship, or you will most likely end up resenting the other person.

Strong boundaries are important in all relationships.

When you are in a healthy relationship, both you and the other person will feel secure in supporting each other's separate interests and encouraging time apart. After all, to totally depend on other people to take care of us is not being in touch with our own inner resources. We all need to have time alone—time to find out who we are, and time to think about our goals and the changes we would like to make for ourselves.

Our alone time can be just as fulfilling as the time we spend with other people—or even more so.

Relationships are wonderful, but they're all temporary, because there comes a time when they end. The one person you are with forever is you. Your relationship with yourself is eternal, so be sure to be your own best friend.

Spend a little time each day connecting with your heart and feeling your love within yourself, as well as going out into the world. The following meditation is a great place to start.

MEDITATION: FEEL THE LOVE

Tune in to that safe place in yourself in which you feel love. You may want to envision your actual heart, or somewhere else. Take a deep breath, and feel the release of your pains and worries and fears. See yourself whole, healthy, and at peace. See yourself filled with love.

Now feel your own love flowing through your body. Literally feel love from the top of your head to the tips of your toes, soaking into every cell of your body.

Know that you are always connected to a Universe that loves you and everyone else unconditionally. This unconditionally loving Universe is the power that created you, and it is always here for you. You can return to that safe place inside yourself anytime you want and feel its loving power.

Now see yourself in a circle of love, and realize that everyone wants the same things. We want to express ourselves creatively in ways that are fulfilling. We want to be peaceful and safe. There is no need to ever be afraid.

In this space, feel your connection with other people in the world. Let the love inside you flow out from heart to heart. And as your love goes out, know that it comes back to you multiplied. Send comforting thoughts to everyone and know that these thoughts are returning to you. See the world becoming an incredible circle of light. Feel that power in every cell of your body. Know that it is available to you anytime. All you need to do is tune in to it.

Journal about what came up for you when you did this meditation.

_____

_____

_____

_____

_____

_____

_____

_____

_____

_____

_____

_____

_____

_____

_____

_____

_____

_____

_____

_____

I am unconditionally loving
and accepting, and I have
a harmonious relationship
with everyone in my life.

WE ALL HAVE FAMILY PATTERNS that have played into how we live our lives and form relationships, even as adults. I'd like you to take some time now to think about your experience with love growing up: How was it a part of your life as a child? How did your parents express love to each other? To you? Was love hidden with fighting, blaming, and pressure? How are things now? Write honestly about all of it, the hugs and affection and the fights and the judgment.

_____

_____

_____

_____

_____

_____

_____

_____

_____

_____

It may be upsetting to see this in writing, but it is helpful to be aware of patterns so that we can break them.

We can always transcend our family's limitations. The first step is to forgive them. We often give the situations and the people in our lives power over us, and these same situations and people keep us mentally trapped. *We* are the ones who suffer when we hold on to old grievances. Forgiveness is the miracle cure for our past pain.

Next, think about what kind of relationship you would like to have with your family members. Turn that into an affirmation, such as: *I am now a complete, secure, independent adult, fully capable of taking care of myself and sharing who I really am with my family.* Start declaring it for yourself, and then find a way to express it to them. This can be done in your mind or written down in your journal, if you are unable to or do not wish to have contact with family members.

You have the right to have the life you want. You have the right to be an empowered adult.

Finally, accept your family members for who they are—not for who you wish they would be. Give love unconditionally, even as you're speaking up for what you want and taking your power back. (If you're not in contact with your family, simply feel that love within your body.) Praise yourself for your courage, and know that you are doing what you need to do to improve all of your relationships.

Write about what happened when you did this.

_____

_____

_____

_____

_____

_____

_____

_____

_____

_____

IT'S IMPORTANT TO CONSIDER our friends when we're talking about relationships. After all, they are often the people who know us the best. We can live without lovers or spouses. We can live without our primary families. But most of us cannot live happily without friends.

I believe that we choose our parents
before we're born into this planet,
but we choose our friends on
a more conscious level.

Think of three events in your life where you were supported by friends. Perhaps a good friend stood up for you or gave you money when you needed it. Maybe they helped you resolve a difficult situation.

In each case, name the event and write down some of the thoughts that preceded each event. Here's an example:

The event: *When people at my first job were making fun of me because I said something stupid at a meeting, Helen stood beside me. She helped me through my embarrassment and became a good, lifelong friend.*

My deepest thoughts were: *Even if I make a mistake, someone will always help me through. I deserve to be supported. I can attract wonderful friends who will stand by me through thick and thin.*

The event:

_____

_____

_____

My deepest thoughts were:

_____

_____

_____

The event:

_____

_____

_____

My deepest thoughts were:

_____

_____

_____

The event:

_____

_____

_____

My deepest thoughts were:

_____

_____

_____

My friends are loving
and supportive.
I give myself permission
to be a friend.

Here are some additional affirmations I like for love and relationships, which you might find helpful:

I feel good about everyone I meet. All my relationships are healthy and supportive.

In any relationship, I can choose the path that makes me happy, whole, and complete.

I am in a joyous, intimate relationship with a person who truly loves me.

Knowing that friends and lovers
were once strangers to me,
I welcome new people into my life.

Try writing down some of your own affirmations here.

_____

_____

_____

_____

_____

_____

_____

_____

_____

_____

_____

_____

_____

_____

_____

_____

_____

_____

_____

_____

_____

_____

_____

_____

Is there anything else you can think of to help you feel more empowered in relationships? Feel free to write, draw, make a collage, or use any creative tool you like.

_____

_____

_____

_____

_____

_____

_____

_____

_____

_____

_____

_____

_____

_____

_____

_____

_____

_____

_____

_____

I now move into a new era of prosperity and abundance.

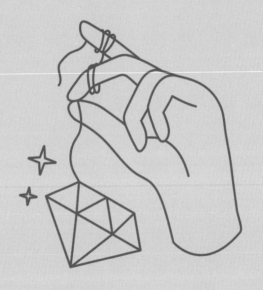

NOW LET'S THINK ABOUT FINANCES. So many people think that all they need to be happy and to fix their problems is money. But we know that there are thousands of people who have a great deal of wealth and still have plenty of problems. Clearly, money does not fix everything.

We all want to be happy and to enjoy peace of mind, but happiness and well-being are an *inside* job. We can have both and still have very little money. It is all about the thoughts we choose to think, the rich or poor conditions we create inside of ourselves.

It is also normal and natural for us to have more money at certain times than others. If we can trust the power within to always take care of us no matter what, we can easily flow through the lean times, knowing that we will have more in the future.

There is so much abundance in this world just waiting for you to experience it!

There is actually more money than you could ever spend, there are more people than you could ever meet, and there is more joy than you could ever imagine—you in fact have everything you need and desire, if only you would believe it. I would like to see you ask for your highest good, and then trust the power within to provide it for you.

ALL OUTER EXPERIENCES reflect inner beliefs. The amount of money we allow ourselves to have has everything to do with our belief system and what we learned about money as children. Many people, for instance, find it difficult to earn more money than their parents. Or so many hold the belief that *If I win the lottery, all my troubles will be over.* This is nonsense. People who win the lottery are often soon worse off than before they won it. That's because they did not have a change of consciousness to go with their newfound wealth. They may not have had the skills to manage their money, but they also didn't believe that they were deserving of it in the first place.

What beliefs do you hold about money?

_____

_____

_____

_____

_____

_____

_____

_____

_____

_____

_____

_____

_____

_____

Are these empowering beliefs, or is it time to make a change? How so?

_____

_____

_____

_____

_____

_____

_____

_____

_____

_____

*The Universe loves to give to us, if only
we feel open to receiving.*

I like to open my arms wide to receive the full measure of prosperity that the Universe offers me. I have always used the affirmation, *My income is constantly increasing.* Another affirmation I like is, *I go beyond my parents' income level.* You have a right to earn more than your parents did. You need to go beyond your feelings of not deserving and accept the abundance of financial wealth that is your Divine right.

Open yourself to receiving good. When something comes into your life, don't push it away, say *Yes!* to it. When you say *Yes!* to your world, opportunity and prosperity will increase a hundredfold.

KEEP IN MIND THAT YOUR JOB is only one of many channels of an infinite source of money. Money can come to you in many ways and from many avenues. No matter how it arrives, accept it with joy as a gift from the Universe.

Gratitude is one of the most empowering things you can do, as appreciation and acceptance act like powerful magnets for miracles every moment of the day. The more we choose to believe in an abundant Universe, the more we find that our needs are met.

Take some time now to write down what you're grateful for in this abundant Universe.

_____

_____

_____

_____

_____

_____

_____

_____

_____

_____

_____

_____

_____

I am filled with
gratitude for all the
blessings in my life.

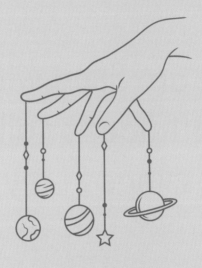

The power of the Universe
backs me in all of my
endeavors, and I have
boundless energy to get
things done easily and quickly.

ASK YOURSELF THE FOLLOWING QUESTION:

What one habit do I need to dissolve to create the financial life I want?

Notice I said *dissolve*, not *break*, the habit. When we break something, the pieces are still around. When we dissolve something, the whole experience disappears. I like to think it goes back to the nothingness from whence it came. Habits come from nowhere, and they can go back to nowhere.

You may discover that you're living in the future, more focused on the good things that might happen, rather than on the reality of what needs to get handled right now. Or you may need to step out of denial and stop pretending that you can continue to spend money when you're unable to take care of the expenses you already have.

What is your habit? And what is the one step you most need to take to improve your financial health?

_____

_____

_____

_____

_____

_____

_____

_____

_____

_____

_____

_____

Next, focus on that one action—preferably the one you've been avoiding—and do something about it within the next 24 hours. You may need to pay your bills, file your taxes, or stop using your credit cards. Or you may need to look for any job that will bring money into your household as soon as possible so you can prepare yourself for more satisfying work later on. Write down what you need to do here.

_____

_____

_____

_____

_____

_____

Make a note to yourself to come back to this page and write about what happened when you did these things. Did this in fact dissolve the habit, or do you have some more work to do?

_____

_____

_____

_____

_____

_____

A WONDERFUL PROSPERITY EXERCISE is to make room for the new. Clean out your refrigerator; get rid of all those little bits of food wrapped in foil. Clean out your closets; get rid of everything you have not used in the last year or so. Sell it, trade it, or give it away.

> The Universe loves symbolic gestures,
> and action is empowering!

Do this clutter-clearing exercise over the next several days, then write about what happened.

_____

_____

_____

_____

_____

_____

_____

_____

_____

_____

_____

_____

_____

_____

_____

_____

Here are some other affirmations for prosperity I like, which you might find helpful:

I joyously give to Life, and
Life lovingly gives to me.

Everything I touch is a success.

My prosperous thoughts
create my prosperous world.

I allow my income to constantly expand,
and I always live in comfort and joy.

Try writing down some of your own affirmations here.

_____

_____

_____

_____

_____

_____

_____

_____

_____

_____

_____

_____

_____

_____

_____

_____

_____

_____

_____

_____

_____

_____

Is there anything else you can think of to help you feel more empowered when it comes to money and prosperity? Feel free to write, draw, make a collage, or use any creative tool you like.

_____

_____

_____

_____

_____

_____

_____

_____

_____

_____

_____

_____

_____

_____

_____

_____

_____

_____

Each day I express
more fully the inner
beauty and strength
of my true being.

NOW LET'S SHIFT OUR ATTENTION to purpose. Who are you? What did you come here to learn? What did you come here to teach?

We all have a unique purpose.

We are more than our personalities, our problems, our fears, and our illnesses. We are far more than our bodies. We are all connected with everyone on the planet and with all of life. We are all spirit, light, energy, vibration, and love, and we all have the power to live our lives with purpose and meaning.

Again, happiness is not something that can be found "out there"; it can only come from within, through self-love and acceptance.

Learn to love yourself and trust the Divine intelligence within you. Changing your mind is the first step to manifesting your best life.

DO YOU KNOW WHAT YOU TRULY WANT to do and how you truly want to feel? Don't start writing immediately with the "right" answer, with what you think you're supposed to want and feel. Be willing to go beyond what you believe today, and consider what genuinely makes you feel alive and inspired.

> Remember, the key to empowerment
> is being true to your authentic self.

It is very important that you align with your individual strengths. If you're not sure what those are, I recommend taking a personality test, such as the Enneagram, to help you figure this out. It's critical that you pursue goals that are true to who you really are, not who you think someone wants you to be. In other words, if you are someone who loves being around people, then being in a room all by yourself probably won't work out. However, if you are someone who likes being alone, then that would be great for you.

Listen to what makes your inner ding say *Yes!* Then think of positive actions that will allow you to feel this way always. Be conscious of your thought patterns, and let go of old beliefs that do not support your better life. Finally, when you find what brings you joy, make sure you do more of it!

Write about what you've learned here.

_____

_____

_____

_____

_____

_____

_____

_____

_____

_____

_____

_____

PERHAPS YOU ARE THINKING of creating your own business, doing charity work, continuing your education, or undertaking another ambitious endeavor. That's wonderful! Just make sure that you don't jump out and start something that you're not completely prepared for or that ultimately won't be right for you.

Once again, listen to your inner ding.

What resources will you need to accomplish your goals? Do you have a community who can assist you with your work or home life? Can you motivate yourself to work if no one is standing over you? New businesses, for example, need long hours of dedication from the owner until there are enough profits to hire some help.

I began my publishing company with one book and one tape. I worked in my bedroom with my 90-year-old mother helping me. We would mail out copies of the book and tape at night. I worked 10-hour days, seven days a week, for a long time. It took me two years before there was enough profit to hire an assistant. It was a nice sideline, but it was a long time before Hay House became a real business.

If you feel called to begin a new business or organization, I advise doing so on a part-time basis first. If you're interested in education, can you take free or part-time classes before enrolling full-time in school? Whatever your passion, try working on aspects of it during your personal time, until you are certain this is what you want to do.

Use this affirmation: *If this enterprise is for my highest good and greatest joy, then let it move forward easily and effortlessly.* Then pay attention to all the signs around you. If delays and obstacles arise, know that this is not the time for you to move forward. If everything falls into place easily, then go for it, but on a part-time basis in the beginning. You can always expand, but it is sometimes hard to retreat.

Remember that you are the only one who is making personal laws for yourself about your career, your path, and your purpose.

You *can* have the life of your dreams!

Think of some affirmations that might help you achieve this, and write them below.

_____

_____

_____

_____

_____

_____

_____

_____

_____

_____

_____

_____

_____

_____

_____

_____

_____

Be sure to declare these affirmations often and focus on what you want.

I release all resistance to expressing my creativity fully.

EACH OF US HAS UNIQUE talents and abilities. Unfortunately, too many of us had well-meaning adults stifle that creativity when we were children. I had a teacher who once told me I couldn't dance because I was too tall. A friend was told he couldn't draw because he drew the wrong tree. It's all so silly. But we were obedient children and believed the messages. Now we can go beyond them.

Another false assumption is that you must be an artist to be creative. That's just one form of creativity, and there are so many more. You're creating every moment of your life—from the most common, ordinary creation of new cells in your body, to your emotional responses, to your relationships, and to your very attitudes about yourself. It's all creativity.

Creativity can be any activity that fulfills you.

You could be a really good bed maker, you could cook delicious food, you could do your job creatively, you could be an artist in the garden, or you could be inventive in the ways in which you're kind to others. These are just a few of the millions of ways of expressing oneself creatively. No matter which way you choose, you'll want to feel satisfaction and be deeply fulfilled by all that you do.

Again, you're expressing yourself creatively every moment of every day. You're being you in your own unique way. Knowing that, you can now release any beliefs that claim you're not creative, and go forward with each and every project that comes to mind.

Give yourself some time to express yourself. If you have children and time is short, find a friend who will help you take care of your children, and vice versa. You both deserve time for yourselves. You are worth it.

What makes you feel creative? What have you always wanted to try?

_____

_____

_____

_____

_____

_____

_____

_____

_____

_____

_____

_____

_____

_____

_____

_____

_____

_____

_____

Listen to your inner ding, and go for it!

I feel good expressing myself in all sorts of creative ways.

Here are some other affirmations I like for purpose, which you might find helpful:

I earn good money doing the things I love.

I work for enjoyment and satisfaction—
not just to earn a living. I use my mind
and thoughts to enhance my life.

My work is deeply fulfilling, and it allows
me to express my creativity freely.

My talents are in demand, and my unique
gifts are appreciated by those around me.

Try writing down some of your own affirmations here.

_____

_____

_____

_____

_____

_____

_____

_____

_____

_____

_____

_____

_____

_____

_____

_____

_____

_____

_____

_____

_____

_____

_____

Is there anything else you can think of to help you feel empowered when it comes to your purpose? Feel free to write, draw, make a collage, or use any creative tool you like.

_____

_____

_____

_____

_____

_____

_____

_____

_____

_____

_____

_____

_____

_____

_____

_____

_____

_____

_____

_____

Are there any other areas in your life in which you're finding it difficult to feel empowered? Write about it here.

_____

_____

_____

_____

_____

_____

_____

_____

_____

_____

_____

_____

_____

_____

_____

_____

_____

_____

_____

_____

_____

Now try to reframe things by creating affirmations or other ideas to bring in the power.

_____

_____

_____

_____

_____

_____

_____

_____

_____

_____

_____

_____

_____

_____

_____

_____

_____

_____

_____

_____

_____

_____

_____

Life brings me only
good experiences.
I am open to new
and wonderful
changes.

WHEN WE ARE REPROGRAMMING our minds, it is normal and natural that we move a little forward, take a step back, and move a little forward again. It is part of practicing. I don't think there is any new skill that you can absolutely master in the first 20 minutes.

Yes, it takes time and practice to learn new ways of thinking. Be patient with yourself.

We often carry beliefs that create our resistance to change.

Maybe you tell yourself, "I can't do that," or, "It's too much work and the time isn't right." Sometimes we may even use others as our excuse to not change or improve our lives. We give our power to "them." We may say, "My family won't let me," or, "The cards are against me," or even, "They have to change before I can." Our excuses really add up.

Don't let your fear or excuses hold you back. *Change is not bad.* Change means that we free ourselves from feelings of isolation, separation, loneliness, anger, fear, and pain. We create lives filled with gratitude and peacefulness, where we can relax and appreciate the things that come to us—where we know that everything will be all right. Affirm:

Everything is all right. It is only change, and I am safe.

It doesn't matter to me which direction my life takes, because I know it's going to be wonderful. Therefore, I can enjoy all sorts of situations and circumstances. I understand that change can be a challenge, but it's worth it. It's uncomfortable and may take some work at first, but you'll get used to the new situation and begin to feel better each day. Those fears and your resistance to change are essentially the same as telling yourself you are not good enough.

The more we embrace change and don't fight it, the more happiness we allow to come into our lives. Choose to no longer be stuck. Begin to take your power back by dissolving the problem you helped to create. Affirm:

> I am willing to release the pattern in my consciousness that is creating this condition.

If you're not ready to make a big change in your life, that's okay. Start with something small. It could be reaching out to an old friend you haven't talked to in a while or taking a walk down a different trail or path than you're used to. You can try a recipe that you've never made before, go to a brand-new workout class, or even make the promise to not complain for the entire day. Just by making these small changes, you rewire your brain and bring in new thoughts.

> These small positive changes will
> help you see your world in a new light.

For the next week, I would like you to try to do something new or make a small change each day. Write about what you did and how you felt about your experience and your day.

_____

_____

_____

_____

_____

_____

_____

_____

_____

_____

_____

_____

_____

_____

_____

_____

_____

_____

_____

_____

_____

I am the only power in my
world, and I create a peaceful,
loving, joyful, fulfilling life.

IN ANY SITUATION, I believe we have the choice between love and fear. Fear is the reason we find it hard to fully embrace our power. We experience fear of change, fear of not changing, fear of the future, and fear of taking a chance. We fear intimacy, and we fear being alone. We may fear letting people know what we need and who we are, and we fear letting go of the past.

As you've learned, what you're thinking is creating the way you feel in your body right now, and it's also creating your experiences for tomorrow. If you're stressing out over every little thing and making mountains out of molehills, you'll never find inner peace or empowerment.

I think that stress is a reaction to life's constant changes. It's an excuse we often use for not taking responsibility for our feelings. Stress is just fear; it's that simple.

> You don't need to be afraid of
> life or your own emotions.

Find out what you're doing to yourself that's creating this fear within you.

Your inner goal is joy, peace, and harmony. Harmony is being at peace with yourself. It's not possible to have stress and inner harmony at the same time. When you're at peace, you do one thing at a time. You don't let things get to you.

In moments of fear, I remember the sun. It is always shining, even though clouds may obscure it for a while. Like the sun, Life is eternally shining its light upon us, even though clouds of negative thinking may temporarily obscure it. When the fears come, we can choose to see them as passing clouds in the sky and let them go on their way.

What do you think? Do you find this image helpful? If not, is there an image that works better for you?

_____

_____

_____

_____

_____

_____

_____

_____

You want to move through life feeling safe. Don't give a little word like *stress* a lot of power. Don't use it as an excuse for creating tension in your body. Nothing—no person, place, or thing—has any power over you. You're the only thinker in your mind, and your thoughts are the ones that create your life. Train yourself to think thoughts that make you feel good. That way, you'll always be creating your life *out* of joy and *in* joy. Joy always brings more to be joyous about.

*Love yourself so that you
can take care of yourself.*

Do everything you can to strengthen your heart, your body, and your mind. Turn to the power within you. When a fearful thought comes up, know that it really is trying to protect you. I suggest that you say to the fear, "I know that you want to protect me. I appreciate that you want to help me. And I thank you." Acknowledge the fearful thought; it's there to take care of you.

When you feel stressed, do something to release the fear. Some great suggestions include breathing deeply, drinking a glass of water, or going for a brisk walk. In fact, I'd like you to take a break and do one of these now and write about how it made you feel.

_____

_____

_____

_____

_____

_____

_____

_____

_____

_____

_____

_____

I now live in
limitless love,
light, and joy.
All is well
in my world.

REPEAT WITH ME: "I live and dwell in the totality of possibilities. Where I am there is all good." Think about these words for a minute. *All good.* Not some, not a little bit, but *all good.*

> When we believe that anything
> is possible, we open ourselves up
> to answers in every area of our life.

That sense of possibility is always up to us individually and collectively. We either have walls around us or we feel safe enough to take them down and allow all good to come to us.

Remember, *loving yourself is the most important thing you can do, because when you love yourself, you are not going to hurt yourself or anyone else.* It's the prescription for world peace. If I don't hurt me and I don't hurt you, how can we have war? The more of us who can get to that place, the better the planet will be. Let's become conscious of what is going on by listening to the words we speak to ourselves and others. Then we can begin to make the changes that will help heal ourselves as well as the rest of the planet. It doesn't really matter where we start as long as we're willing to start.

> We *always* have the power to make a change.

When you know that Life loves you, and that you live in a friendly Universe, it helps you in both the good times and the bad times. When you trust in love, it's impossible to feel alone. Love introduces you to the totality of possibilities. It opens you up to a power that knows what's best for you. It leads you to your true self and your highest good. Love will show you the way.

Now, return once again to what you wrote on pages 7 and 55. Take some time to imagine that you have or do or are whatever you want. In as much detail as you can, visualize the things that fill you with passion and enthusiasm. Really let your mind get creative to bring this picture to life, and have fun!

Write down your empowering vision here.

_____

_____

_____

_____

_____

_____

_____

_____

_____

_____

_____

_____

_____

_____

_____

_____

_____

Next, see yourself actually living the life you just created in the previous exercise. What does this ideal life feel like? What do you look like? What do you feel, see, taste, touch, or hear? Imagine your relationships. Who are you associating with? How does it feel to have released the past, ready to make the rest of your life the best of your life?

_____

_____

_____

_____

_____

_____

_____

_____

_____

_____

_____

_____

_____

_____

_____

Relax and breathe in your newfound freedom and happiness.

AS WE WRAP UP HERE, I'd like to leave you with a special affirmation. I suggest you say it to yourself in the mirror, or at least post it somewhere you can see it often.

I accept all that I have created for myself. I love and accept myself exactly as I am. I support myself, trust myself, and accept myself wherever I am. I can be within the love of my own heart. I place my hand over my heart and feel the love that is there. I know there is plenty of room for me to accept myself right here and now. I accept my body and my experiences. I accept all that I have created for myself— my past and my present. I am willing to allow my future to happen. I am a Divine, magnificent expression of Life, and I deserve the very best. I accept this for myself now. I accept miracles. I accept healing. I accept wholeness. And most of all, I accept myself. I am precious, and I cherish who I am. All is truly well in my world.

Here is a list of some of the most powerful thoughts that have been woven throughout this journal:

Life is very simple.

What you put your attention on grows.

The point of power is in the present moment.

It is only a thought, and a
thought can be changed.

You *always* have a choice.

All the answers to all the questions
you will ever ask are already within you.

Do not think your mind is in control.
You are in control of your mind.

The Universe loves a grateful person.

Every experience is an opportunity for growth.

It may be a good idea to post this list where you can see it, so you can always be encouraged to remember the power you have to change your life, no matter what.

ABOUT THE AUTHOR

Louise Hay was an inspirational teacher who educated millions since the 1984 publication of her bestseller *You Can Heal Your Life*, which has more than 50 million copies in print worldwide. Renowned for demonstrating the power of affirmations to bring about positive change, Louise was the author of more than 30 books for adults and children, including the bestsellers *The Power Is Within You* and *Heal Your Body*. In addition to her books, Louise produced numerous audio and video programs, card decks, online courses, and other resources for leading a healthy, joyous, and fulfilling life.

Websites: **www.louisehay.com, www.healyourlife.com, and www.facebook.com/louiselhay**

ALSO BY LOUISE HAY

BOOKS

All Is Well
(with Mona Lisa Schulz, M.D., Ph.D.)

The Bone Broth Secret
(with Heather Dane)

Colors & Numbers

Experience Your Good Now!

Heal Your Body
(also available in Spanish)

Heal Your Mind
(with Mona Lisa Schulz, M.D., Ph.D.)

Heart Thoughts

I Can Do It®
(book-with-download)

I Think, I Am!
(children's book with Kristina Tracy)

Life Loves You
(with Robert Holden)

Love Your Body

Love Yourself, Heal Your Life Workbook

Meditations to Heal Your Life
(also available in Spanish)

Mirror Work

The Power Is Within You
(also available in Spanish)

Trust Life

You Can Create an Exceptional Life
(with Cheryl Richardson, also available in Spanish)

You Can Heal Your Heart
(with David Kessler)

You Can Heal Your Life
(also available in a gift edition and in Spanish)

You Can Heal Your Life Companion Book

AUDIO PROGRAMS

All Is Well (audiobook)

Anger Releasing

Cancer

Change and Transition

Dissolving Barriers

Embracing Change

Evening Meditation

Feeling Fine Affirmations

Forgiveness/Loving the Inner Child

Heal Your Mind (audiobook)

How to Love Yourself (audiobook)

I Can Do It® (audiobook)

Life Loves You (audiobook)

Love Your Body (audiobook)

Meditations for Loving Yourself to Great Health

Meditations for Personal Healing

Morning and Evening Meditations

101 Power Thoughts

Overcoming Fears (audiobook)

The Power Is Within You (audiobook)

The Power of Your Spoken Word

Receiving Prosperity

Self-Esteem Affirmations (subliminal)

Self-Healing

Stress-Free (subliminal)

*Subliminal Affirmations
for Positive Self-Esteem*

Totality of Possibilities

What I Believe and Deep Relaxation

You Can Heal Your Heart (audiobook)

You Can Heal Your Life
(audiobook, also available in Spanish)

You Can Heal Your Life Study Course

VIDEOS

Dissolving Barriers

Doors Opening

*Painting the Future: Tales of
Everyday Magic*

Receiving Prosperity

You Can Heal Your Life, the movie
(available in standard and
expanded editions)

You Can Trust Your Life
(with Cheryl Richardson)

INSPIRATIONAL CARDS

Heart Thoughts Cards

How to Love Yourself Cards

I Can Do It®︎ Cards

Life Loves You Cards (with Robert
Holden)

Louise Hay's Affirmations for Self-Esteem

Love Your Body Cards

Power Thought Cards (original and
keepsake editions)

JOURNALS

*The Gift of Gratitude: A Guided Journal
for Counting Your Blessings*

*How to Love Yourself: A Guided Journal
for Discovering Your Inner Strength and
Beauty*

CALENDAR

I Can Do It®︎ Calendar
(for each individual year)

ONLINE COURSES

*Loving Yourself: 21 Days to Improved
Self-Esteem with Mirror Work*
(with Robert Holden)

*You Can Trust Your Life: Create Your
Best Year Yet* (with Cheryl Richardson)

All of the above are available at your local
bookstore, or may be ordered by visiting:

Hay House USA: www.hayhouse.com®︎
Hay House Australia: www.hayhouse.com.au
Hay House UK: www.hayhouse.co.uk
Hay House India: www.hayhouse.co.in

***

HAY HOUSE TITLES
OF RELATED INTEREST

YOU CAN HEAL YOUR LIFE, the movie,
starring Louise Hay & Friends
(available as an online streaming video)
www.hayhouse.com/louise-movie

THE SHIFT, the movie,
starring Dr. Wayne W. Dyer
(available as an online streaming video)
www.hayhouse.com/the-shift-movie

The Cosmic Journal
by Yanik Silver

The High Performance Journal
by Brendon Burchard

The Letting Go Guided Journal
by Dr. David R. Hawkins, M.D., Ph.D.

Living Your Purpose Journal
by Dr. Wayne W. Dyer

Positive Manifestation Journal
by the Editors of Hay House

Super Attractor Journal
by Gabrielle Bernstein

3 Minute Positivity Journal
by Kristen Butler

All of the above are available at your local bookstore,
or may be ordered by contacting Hay House (see next page).